Samuel French Acting Edition

Thespian Playworks 2019

All Things Considered
by Breanna Spink

Ismene
by Gabi Garcia

Memories of Vichy
by Samuel Kaplan

Silent Night
by Sarah Lina Sparks

All Things Considered Copyright © 2020 by Breanna Spink
Ismene Copyright © 2020 by Gabi Garcia
Memories of Vichy Copyright © 2020 by Samuel Kaplan
Silent Night Copyright © 2020 by Sarah Lina Sparks
All Rights Reserved

THESPIAN PLAYWORKS 2019 is fully protected under the copyright laws of the United States of America, the British Commonwealth, including Canada, and all member countries of the Berne Convention for the Protection of Literary and Artistic Works, the Universal Copyright Convention, and/or the World Trade Organization conforming to the Agreement on Trade Related Aspects of Intellectual Property Rights. All rights, including professional and amateur stage productions, recitation, lecturing, public reading, motion picture, radio broadcasting, television and the rights of translation into foreign languages are strictly reserved.

ISBN 978-0-573-70851-0

www.concordtheatricals.com
www.concordtheatricals.co.uk

FOR PRODUCTION ENQUIRIES

UNITED STATES AND CANADA
info@concordtheatricals.com
1-866-979-0447

UNITED KINGDOM AND EUROPE
licensing@concordtheatricals.co.uk
020-7054-7200

Each title is subject to availability from Concord Theatricals, depending upon country of performance. Please be aware that *THESPIAN PLAYWORKS 2019* may not be licensed by Concord Theatricals in your territory. Professional and amateur producers should contact the nearest Concord Theatricals office or licensing partner to verify availability.

CAUTION: Professional and amateur producers are hereby warned that *THESPIAN PLAYWORKS 2019* is subject to a licensing fee. Publication of this play(s) does not imply availability for performance. Both amateurs and professionals considering a production are strongly advised to apply to Concord Theatricals before starting rehearsals, advertising, or booking a theater. A licensing fee must be paid whether the title(s) is presented for charity or gain and whether or not admission is charged. Professional/Stock licensing fees are quoted upon application to Concord Theatricals.

This work is published by Samuel French, an imprint of Concord Theatricals.

No one shall make any changes in this title(s) for the purpose of production. No part of this book may be reproduced, stored in a retrieval system, or transmitted in any form, by any means, now known or yet to be invented, including mechanical, electronic, photocopying, recording, videotaping, or otherwise, without the prior written permission of the publisher. No one shall upload this title(s), or part of this title(s), to any social media websites.

For all enquiries regarding motion picture, television, and other media rights, please contact Concord Theatricals.

MUSIC USE NOTE

Licensees are solely responsible for obtaining formal written permission from copyright owners to use copyrighted music in the performance of this play and are strongly cautioned to do so. If no such permission is obtained by the licensee, then the licensee must use only original music that the licensee owns and controls. Licensees are solely responsible and liable for all music clearances and shall indemnify the copyright owners of the play(s) and their licensing agent, Concord Theatricals, against any costs, expenses, losses and liabilities arising from the use of music by licensees. Please contact the appropriate music licensing authority in your territory for the rights to any incidental music.

IMPORTANT BILLING AND CREDIT REQUIREMENTS

If you have obtained performance rights to this title, please refer to your licensing agreement for important billing and credit requirements.

ABOUT THESPIAN PLAYWORKS

Thespian Playworks is a writing contest and script-development program for high school students, sponsored by the Educational Theatre Association and run by the staff of *Dramatics* magazine. Each year, up to four finalists are invited to the International Thespian Festival, where the students work with a professional director, a dramaturg, and a volunteer cast of actors to put their short plays on their feet before a live audience.

Launched in 1994 as a tribute to longtime International Thespian Society executive Doug Finney, the program aims to nurture young playwrights, and over Playworks' history, many participants have gone on to college majors and careers in theatre, writing, and related fields. Whatever the eventual future of the writers or their scripts, Playworks is an exhilarating experience in a creative discipline seldom taught in schools or celebrated in the wider culture.

The call for entries goes out each fall, with submission deadlines in midwinter. *Dramatics* receives scores of scripts from high school Thespians all over the U.S., Canada, and as far away as the United Arab Emirates. Each play is reviewed at least twice, as teams of readers (including *Dramatics* staff and other professional critics and theatre artists) narrow down the entries: first to a dozen semifinalists, then to the final four. Each semifinalist receives a personal letter with feedback on his or her script.

For more on Thespian Playworks, please visit www.schooltheatre.org/nextgenerationworks.

CONTENTS

All Things Considered. 7
Ismene 23
Memories of Vichy. 37
Silent Night. 59

ALL THINGS CONSIDERED

Breanna Spink

ALL THINGS CONSIDERED by Breanna Spink of Troupe 4101 at Lake Dallas High School in Corinth, Texas was presented in a staged reading as part of the Thespian Playworks program, sponsored by Concord Theatricals, at the 2019 International Thespian Festival on June 29, 2019. The production was directed by Carolyn Greer, with dramaturgy by Nicholas Pappas. The stage manager was Carley Ballard. The cast was as follows:

LEIGH	Mariah Williams
BRYAN	Bryson Schultz
YOUNG LEIGH / LEIGH'S THERAPIST	Alliyah Jeter
YOUNG BRYAN / BRYAN'S THERAPIST	Jared Cotrufo

CHARACTERS

LEIGH – Twenty-two years old. The typical teen movie protagonist. Edgy, witty, and depressed. After the death of her son, she is unable to think of anything else, ignoring all other parts of her life, including Bryan.

BRYAN – Twenty-two years old. Leigh's fiancé and adoptive father of her son. As the one to watch their son die, he finds himself unable to think about the loss at all.

YOUNG LEIGH / LEIGH'S THERAPIST – Trying to navigate a world that has never been kind to her. Doubles as Leigh's no-nonsense therapist.

YOUNG BRYAN / BRYAN'S THERAPIST – The "gentle giant," caring but often hypocritical and too quick to sacrifice his happiness. Doubles as Bryan's understanding but straightforward therapist.

AUTHOR'S NOTES

At several points in this play, Leigh and Bryan are onstage together with their dialogue overlapping. It's important to note that they are never actually in the same room and are not interacting with each other until the final scene. Therapist characters represent embodiments of the characters' past selves, and therefore should be played by the actors portraying Young Leigh and Young Bryan.

(Lights up. A single light, which represents the grave of Leigh and Bryan's son, shines center stage. **LEIGH** *approaches it slowly. She looks disgruntled, wearing loose, comfortable clothing.)*

LEIGH. Hey, kiddo. I... I don't know what to do here. I'm supposed to be talking, but I don't know what to say. My therapist suggested I do this so I can be honest with myself. With you. You're the one person I could never lie to. So, honestly, I would rather be dead than standing here.

YOUNG LEIGH. *(Offstage.)* There's no one to judge you or give unwanted input. That is what you wanted, right?

LEIGH. *(To the grave.)* Kind of morbid if you ask me.

YOUNG LEIGH. Are you listening, Leigh?

(The scene transitions to **LEIGH***'s earlier conversation with her therapist, portrayed by* **YOUNG LEIGH**.*)*

LEIGH'S THERAPIST. This is not permission to allow yourself to fall into negativity. Remember, you're not talking to yourself, you're talking to him.

LEIGH. You told me I wasn't supposed to visit him.

LEIGH'S THERAPIST. I did, but it was only because you would refuse to leave. You've made progress since then.

LEIGH. Oh, and this is my reward?

LEIGH'S THERAPIST. It's the next step in your healing process.

LEIGH. How do you know this won't just trigger some kind of relapse?

LEIGH'S THERAPIST. Honestly, I don't.

LEIGH. That's reassuring.

LEIGH'S THERAPIST. Exposure Therapy is a fairly new form of treatment, but studies have shown it can help those dealing with prolonged grief.

LEIGH. Prolonged? It's been ten months.

LEIGH'S THERAPIST. Symptoms such as yours that persist for longer than six months are considered prolonged.

LEIGH. Oh, my God.

LEIGH'S THERAPIST. I'm asking you to take a chance.

LEIGH. What am I supposed to say? Where do I start?

> (*Transition to* **BRYAN**'s *conversation with his therapist, portrayed by* **YOUNG BRYAN**.)

BRYAN'S THERAPIST. Let's start with how you're feeling.

BRYAN. Fine. (*Realizing this likely won't cut it with his therapist.*) I'm worried about Leigh. She's barely eating, I don't think she's sleeping, and she's barely left the house. I know she's grieving but...

BRYAN'S THERAPIST. How are you feeling, Bryan?

BRYAN. I'm worried.

BRYAN'S THERAPIST. About Leigh.

BRYAN. Of course.

> (*At some point,* **LEIGH** *has returned to the grave.*)

LEIGH. I know I shouldn't blame myself. I know logically it's not my fault. I've talked to the doctors. I've been to the support groups and the sermons. But no matter how many times I hear it, there'll always be part of me that wonders what I could have done differently. I've started to hate myself. I look at my reflection, and I just see a failure.

BRYAN. It's always a gamble with her. I never know what version of her is going to wake up next to me in the morning. If she's there at all.

LEIGH. There are some days when I wake up and it's not so bad. Then one thing happens, and I get sent spiraling. Sometimes it's kids playing down the street. The other day it was a shirt in the mall. It had constellations on it. Like the ones we put on your ceiling with the glow-in-the-dark stars. These things can remind me of you. And everything that reminds me of you hurts.

BRYAN'S THERAPIST. How long have you known Leigh?

BRYAN. Since middle school. I met her in fourth-period math class. On the first day of school, this girl walked right up to me and said that she knew I was a football player, but if I was planning on picking on her, like some of the other guys on the team, I should know that she could probably beat me up. I instantly had a crush on her.

BRYAN'S THERAPIST. Is that when you started dating?

BRYAN. No, we were just friends. We became incredibly close, though. Eventually, it didn't matter if we were dating or not. I just enjoyed hanging out with her. When we got to high school, she started dating other guys, but I didn't mind because at least most guys treated her well.

BRYAN'S THERAPIST. Most guys?

BRYAN. There was this...dick. She met him right before homecoming our sophomore year. I tried to tell Leigh that I didn't like the guy the first time I met him. But she said I just didn't know him and told me he had been so sweet when he asked her to homecoming... Leigh wasn't usually big on dances, but that year she was so excited. Then, the night of the dance, the guy bails on her for another girl because Leigh wouldn't put out. I had never seen her that upset. Her grandmother called me saying she couldn't get Leigh out of her room.

BRYAN'S THERAPIST. How did you feel?

BRYAN. Angry. No, beyond that. I didn't see how anyone could do that to her. I wanted to confront the guy, but I knew it would've ended in a fight. Sure, I probably could've taken him, but I wasn't a huge fan of physical violence. So, instead, I went home, dug out the cash I had been saving for a car, and rented a tuxedo.

(**YOUNG BRYAN** *enters, now wearing a tuxedo. He approaches the bedroom door. On the other side of the door,* **YOUNG LEIGH** *has entered at some point, wearing her dress.*)

YOUNG BRYAN. *(Knocking on the door of Leigh's bedroom.)* Leigh?

YOUNG LEIGH. Go away, Bryan.

YOUNG BRYAN. Leigh, open the door and get dressed. You're going to be late.

YOUNG LEIGH. Bryan, I'm not going.

YOUNG BRYAN. Why not? You have a dress, a ride...you have a date.

YOUNG LEIGH. I got dumped, remember? You were right about everything. So, if you don't mind, I'd rather spend the rest of the night wallowing.

YOUNG BRYAN. Are you really going to let that dickhead ruin your night?

YOUNG LEIGH. Yes.

YOUNG BRYAN. When have you ever let some jerk keep you from having fun? You're stronger than that, Leigh. So please, put on your dress, which I was dragged to five different stores to find and never even got to see, and let me take my best friend to the dance.

(**YOUNG LEIGH** *says nothing.* **YOUNG BRYAN** *assumes she's turning him down and begins to walk away, until she finally opens the door.*)

Wow.

YOUNG LEIGH. Shut up.

YOUNG BRYAN. No, really. Wow.

(The young couple freezes.)

BRYAN. That was the night I realized that I loved her. Dancing with her, seeing her laugh...being the one to make her laugh. You know those moments in cheesy romance movies where the two leads are in a crowded room, but when they see each other for the first time everyone else disappears? That's what it felt like when we were dancing. Just us together.

LEIGH. You never realize how sudden death is. One day there's an entire life in your arms. Full of potential and joy and hope. And you hold on to this life for two years, but it barely seems like any time has passed. Then one day there's a hospital. There's a doctor saying nothing can be done. Then there's nothing. When two years turn into a literal lifetime, time stops making sense. A few minutes turns into eternity, and then you blink and another ten months have flown by and suddenly you're twenty-two and you've seen five different therapists trying desperately to get better because even breathing became difficult.

(**BRYAN** *enters.*)

I'm still trying to hold on to that life. To you. I blame Bryan for ever giving me hope. For staying when I've tried so hard to push him away. He feels he must be strong for his broken mess of a fiancée, but that makes everything worse.

BRYAN. I tried to stay. After we graduated. I was going to turn down the scholarship at Ohio State so I could stay in Washington with Leigh. I wanted to marry her.

LEIGH. He loves me so much. Too much.

BRYAN. We could've gone to Washington State together. Their football team is fine.

LEIGH. I hate him for it.

BRYAN. But she wouldn't let me. She threatened to break up with me the moment I told her.

(**YOUNG LEIGH** *enters, followed by* **YOUNG BRYAN**.)

YOUNG BRYAN. Leigh, can we talk about this, please?
YOUNG LEIGH. There's nothing to talk about.
YOUNG BRYAN. I made my decision –

YOUNG LEIGH. It was a stupid decision! What if we break up?

YOUNG BRYAN. We're not going to break up.

YOUNG LEIGH. That's not entirely up to you. You never even thought to ask me if I would be willing to go with you.

YOUNG BRYAN. I could never let you do that.

YOUNG LEIGH. How do you not see how hypocritical that is?

YOUNG BRYAN. It would never work anyways. Think of the money.

YOUNG LEIGH. Maybe not, but that's not the point I'm trying to make. I would spend every day living in guilt because you walked out on the chance of a lifetime for me. I know, ultimately, I have no control over what you do. If you go, we can try this long-distance thing.

YOUNG BRYAN. If I don't go?

YOUNG LEIGH. If you don't go, it's over for us.

BRYAN. She left it up to me, but there was never really a choice. So, I left to pursue my dream. I had a full-ride scholarship for football at Ohio State. One of the best college teams in the country. I'm sorry, I didn't mean to stray so far off-topic.

BRYAN'S THERAPIST. Considering the conversation is supposed to be about you, I think that's the most on-topic you've been since we started these sessions.

(**LEIGH** *enters.*)

LEIGH. I was nineteen. It hadn't been that long since Bryan and I decided we couldn't do long distance.

BRYAN'S THERAPIST. You and Leigh broke up after you left for college, right?

BRYAN. I knew it was hurting her. It was hurting me too. We just kept growing apart.

LEIGH. I went to a party. I didn't even like to party, but I felt so alone for the first time in years. I needed a distraction, and I found one in a handsome boy with blue eyes. I couldn't pick him out of a lineup now if I tried.

BRYAN. Leigh stopped talking to me for weeks. No warning. She just...disappeared.

LEIGH. I didn't know how to tell Bryan when I found out I was pregnant. So soon after he had left... I couldn't do that to him.

BRYAN. At first, I thought she just wanted space but after a while without contact, I got scared. Eventually, I called her grandmother. When she told me Leigh was pregnant, I knew I had to go back. I had to be with her.

LEIGH. There was no way I could raise a child on my own. I was going to give you up for adoption. I should have done what was best for you. But I wasn't strong enough then. And now...I'm not even strong enough to get better. I've been blaming everyone for this rock on my chest that keeps me from taking a breath and letting go, but the truth is I'm the one who's afraid to move on because it means accepting that I really did screw up and that you're actually –

(She chokes on her words.)

BRYAN'S THERAPIST. How are you, Bryan?

BRYAN. Leigh wasn't getting out of bed this morning.

BRYAN'S THERAPIST. How are you?

BRYAN. She's barely talking to me.

BRYAN'S THERAPIST. How are you?

BRYAN. You're supposed to be helping! This isn't helping.

BRYAN'S THERAPIST. Who isn't this helping, Bryan?

BRYAN. Leigh.

BRYAN'S THERAPIST. Leigh isn't here. Who isn't this helping?

BRYAN. Me! OK? Is that what you want to hear? This isn't helping me.

BRYAN'S THERAPIST. It's not about what I want to hear. I can't treat you until you decide you deserve to be treated. Your son passed away, and not once have you told me how you're feeling about it.

BRYAN. If you ask Leigh, she'd say he wasn't my son.

BRYAN'S THERAPIST. What do you say?

BRYAN. It doesn't matter. His dad was some frat boy that hooked up with Leigh at a party.

BRYAN'S THERAPIST. But you were the one that took care of him, weren't you? You were the one that stayed in the hospital room. This isn't about Leigh –

BRYAN. Leigh is the one who's grieving. Leigh is the one who won't leave the house unless I force her to. Leigh is the one who needs this.

BRYAN'S THERAPIST. What do you need?

BRYAN. I need a fiancée who gets out of bed on her own.

BRYAN'S THERAPIST. I don't think you do.

BRYAN. You're right. I need you to get the fuck out of my head.

(He gets up to exit.)

BRYAN'S THERAPIST. Bryan –

BRYAN. No! No. I don't need you. Leigh doesn't need you. I can fix this. I can help her. I can –

BRYAN'S THERAPIST. No, you can't.

BRYAN. What?

BRYAN'S THERAPIST. You cannot fix her. The choice to heal is one that she has to make on her own. You can be there for her. You can support her. You can work with her. But you can't fix her. People aren't machines.

BRYAN. I don't know what else I can do.

BRYAN'S THERAPIST. You can focus on what you need first.

BRYAN. I need –

BRYAN'S THERAPIST. You need to let go, Bryan.

*(**BRYAN** searches for his excuse. Unable to find one, he gives in.)*

BRYAN. I get these nightmares. At least once a week if not more. I dream about that day in the hospital room, sitting by his side. Talking to him... I should go.

BRYAN'S THERAPIST. You made progress today, Bryan.

*(**BRYAN** begins to exit.)*

I think you should talk to your fiancée.

> (**BRYAN** *says nothing and exits fully. Somewhere during this exchange,* **LEIGH** *has entered, followed by* **YOUNG LEIGH** *and* **YOUNG BRYAN**.*)*

LEIGH. It was late when Bryan showed up at my door. Close to midnight, I think. He looked like a mess because he had just run over from the airport. I tried to go outside to meet him, but as soon as I opened the front door, he had already dropped down onto his knee.

YOUNG BRYAN. Marry me.

YOUNG LEIGH. Bryan, what the hell are you doing here?

YOUNG BRYAN. I know you're pregnant.

YOUNG LEIGH. It's not –

YOUNG BRYAN. I know it's not mine. I don't care. Whatever you choose to do with this baby, I wanted to be here for it. I wanted to be here for you.

YOUNG LEIGH. That's sweet and all, Bryan, but why are you proposing?

YOUNG BRYAN. Because I love you. If you decide to give this kid up, I'm going to support you. If you keep it, I want to help you raise it. I want to give you a family.

> (**LEIGH** *turns to address her son again.*)

LEIGH. I wanted to be angry with him for coming back and trying to rescue me again. I wanted to tell him no and send him back to Ohio. But I had turned him away once and my life fell apart. I didn't want to give you up for adoption, but I had no other choice. Bryan gave me a choice. He gave me hope. I needed him. I didn't want to, but I did. I *do*.

> (**BRYAN** *enters.*)

BRYAN. Hey.

LEIGH. What are you doing here?

BRYAN. I wanted to pick you up.

LEIGH. I told you I would walk.

BRYAN. I know but I was on my way home and –

LEIGH. I have twenty more minutes here.

BRYAN. I'll wait.

LEIGH. I'm supposed to be alone. That's part of this. Just go home, Bryan.

BRYAN. At least let me wait in the car.

LEIGH. It's a five-minute walk! What do you think is going to happen?

BRYAN. I think I've earned the right to be a little worried.

LEIGH. You're always so damn worried!

BRYAN. Someone has to be.

LEIGH. If I'm such a burden to you, then why are you still here? Why haven't you left me yet?

BRYAN. Do you really think I could just leave and forget about this? About you? I care about you. I love you.

LEIGH. You've always had to be the one to swoop in to save the day.

BRYAN. Because I don't know how to do anything else!

LEIGH. Stop using love as an excuse to treat me like a child. Homecoming, college, your proposal, you never consulted me on anything.

BRYAN. Every time you push me away, it feels like a knife in my chest.

LEIGH. This isn't about me. My son...

BRYAN. *(Speaking over her.)* Our son. Our son.

LEIGH. – Is dead and all you can think about is me. Do you miss him? Do you even remember him?

BRYAN. *(Loud enough to cut her off.)* Our son.

LEIGH. What?

BRYAN. He was our son.

LEIGH. Then why have you never acted like it?

BRYAN. I watched him die, Leigh. I was alone in that hospital room with him while he died. You were in the car.

LEIGH. You can't blame me –

BRYAN. Why not? That's all you ever do to me. You would have hated me if I followed you. What did you want me to do?

LEIGH. I don't know! OK? I don't. I wasn't strong enough to hold Noah when he needed me the most. They kept saying it wasn't our fault. They said –

BRYAN. Respiratory infections are so common, but he was already developing asthma.

YOUNG BRYAN. Hey, Noah.

BRYAN. We couldn't have known.

YOUNG BRYAN. I'm here, OK? I want you to know that I'm here.

LEIGH. Kids get colds, and that's what it seemed like. Everyone told us not to worry every time we brought it up.

BRYAN. But he didn't get better. He didn't stop coughing. Then one morning he stopped breathing.

YOUNG BRYAN. I don't know what to say here, kiddo. Don't be afraid. I'm afraid. But you're so much braver than me.

BRYAN. There was nothing we could do. Nothing I could do.

LEIGH. You stayed. I couldn't stay. I thought it would be easier to just walk away and accept that he died rather than watching it happen.

BRYAN. All I did was comfort him. It didn't seem real. I didn't want it to be real.

LEIGH. Why didn't you ever cry? You came out of the hospital and you drove us home, then you put me to bed and the entire time, you refused to cry. Why didn't you cry?

BRYAN. When we got home and I held you, I could feel you pulling away and all I could think about was losing you too. I kept imagining coming home and finding out you had left me or finding you –

(Pause.)

I felt helpless all over again. But as long as you let me hold you, it was enough.

*(He reaches for **LEIGH**, but she pulls away.)*

BRYAN. Because being strong for you meant I didn't have to feel like you.

LEIGH. I didn't want you to be strong. I wanted you to be there with me, not there for me. I still do. I want to learn to love you again.

BRYAN. I –

LEIGH. We'll talk about this at home, I promise. But you have to let me get there on my own.

BRYAN. OK… OK.

LEIGH. Where will you go?

BRYAN. Home, if that's what you want.

LEIGH. I – Thank you.

> (**BRYAN** *exits.* **LEIGH** *turns back to address her son.*)

I don't know how to say goodbye. I don't think I…we ever will. But I think we're going to be OK.

End of Play

ISMENE

Gabi Garcia

ISMENE was presented in May 2019 as part of the 2019 One-Acts Festival at Sunset High School in Portland, Oregon. The production was directed by Gabi Garcia. The stage manager was Presley Rehling-Manullang. The cast was as follows:

ISMENE..................................... Annika Zomerman
CREON.. Jasper Warhus
TEIRESIAS.. Jason Bube
ANTIGONE...................................... Madison Pearce
HAEMON ....Jack Pedro
EURYDICE ....Samantha Reinhold

ISMENE was presented in a staged reading as part of the Thespian Playworks program at the 2019 International Thespian Festival, sponsored by Concord Theatricals, on June 29, 2019. The production was directed by Bill Myatt, with dramaturgy by Mark Kaufmann. The stage manager was Lauren Porter. The cast was as follows:

ISMENE... Bellah Crawford
CREON... Atticus Brunner
TEIRESIAS.. Joshua Lester
ANTIGONE...Dale Tanner
HAEMON .... Ben Susskind
EURYDICE .... Christina Jesenski

CHARACTERS

ISMENE – seventeen, naive, lost
CREON – middle-aged, guilty, tired
TEIRESIAS – elderly, out of his mind
ANTIGONE – fifteen, intelligent, pragmatic
HAEMON – sixteen, vengeful
EURYDICE – middle-aged, wise

SETTING

Antigone and Ismene's childhood nursery

TIME

Any time

PRONUCIATION GUIDE

Antigone [an-TIH-guh-nee]
Creon [KREE-on]
Eteocles [eh-TAY-oh-klees]
Eurydice [yuh-RIH-dih-see]
Haemon [HAY-muhn]
Ismene [IS-men-ee]
Polynices [PAHL-ih-nai-sees]
Teiresias [tai-REE-see-uhs]

AUTHOR'S NOTES

The fractured dialogue is spoken as if the six Chorus members were one person, that is, continuously and without pause until the period marking the end of the sentence. Actors are part of the Chorus until noted that they step out as specific characters.

A slash (/) in the middle of dialogue indicates when the next character begins speaking.

(The nursery crumbles around the scene. Shadows fill the formerly bright and sunny space. A well-loved rocking chair sits to the side. **ISMENE, CREON, TEIRESIAS, ANTIGONE, HAEMON,** *and* **EURYDICE,** *cloaked as the six-person* **CHORUS,** *cluster together.)*

CHORUS. *(Chanting or singing.)* The walls
ISMENE. *(Whispering.)* echo
ANTIGONE, HAEMON & TEIRESIAS. with the
CREON. past
ANTIGONE, HAEMON, EURYDICE & TEIRESIAS. of this place.
CREON, HAEMON & TEIRESIAS. The young king
ISMENE, ANTIGONE & EURYDICE. and his wife-mother,
CHORUS. felled by fate.
ANTIGONE. A kingdom
CHORUS. split by divided sons slain on each other's blade.
CHORUS (EXCEPT CREON). The uncle,
CREON. unwillingly bound
CHORUS (EXCEPT CREON). to the kingdom.
ANTIGONE. The honorable princess
CHORUS (EXCEPT ANTIGONE). fighting for her death.
HAEMON. The prince in mourning,
EURYDICE. his mother grief-stricken.
TEIRESIAS. The blind seer bridges both sides.
ISMENE. And the sister.
CHORUS (EXCEPT ISMENE). Left behind.
CHORUS. These are our players.
TEIRESIAS. Even in death they do not part. The treasonous
ISMENE & CREON. treasonous
ANTIGONE & HAEMON. treasonous

EURYDICE & TEIRESIAS. treasonous

TEIRESIAS. princess

CHORUS (EXCEPT ANTIGONE). Antigone

ANTIGONE. has buried Polynices against her uncle Creon's will.

CREON. Creon does not want her to

CHORUS. die

TEIRESIAS. by his hand.

ISMENE. Ismene waits.

ANTIGONE. Antigone coerces Creon into submission,

TEIRESIAS. ensuring

ISMENE, HAEMON & EURYDICE. her death.

CREON. The king is

TEIRESIAS. powerless

CREON. to stop her.

ISMENE. She is

TEIRESIAS. trapped

CREON, ANTIGONE, HAEMON & EURYDICE. in a cave of her

CHORUS. fate.

HAEMON. Haemon has

TEIRESIAS. slipped

ANTIGONE. in with her.

EURYDICE. Eurydice, Creon's wife,

TEIRESIAS. self-slain

ISMENE, CREON, ANTIGONE & HAEMON. by her own knitting needles.

TEIRESIAS. Creon is too late. Ismene waits.

HAEMON & TEIRESIAS. She is dead.

ANTIGONE & EURYDICE. He is dead.

CREON, ANTIGONE & HAEMON. Ismene waits.

CREON, ANTIGONE, HAEMON & EURYDICE. Ismene waits.

*(***TEIRESIAS** *cackles from the* **CHORUS**.*)*

CHORUS (EXCEPT ISMENE). Ismene waits.

CREON, ANTIGONE & HAEMON. Ismene waits.
ANTIGONE & TEIRESIAS. Ismene waits.

> (**ISMENE**, *removing her cloak, steps out of the* **CHORUS**.)

ISMENE. Ismene waits.

> *(Silence.)*

Where is she... Where is she... Where is she...

> *(Silence. A drum rings out, and* **TEIRESIAS** *laughs from the* **CHORUS**.)

Antigone?

> (**ANTIGONE** *steps out of the* **CHORUS**. *Another drum rings out, farther away.*)

NO!!

> *(A third drum rings out in the distance as* **TEIRESIAS** *steps out of the* **CHORUS** *and into the rocking chair.* **CREON** *screams from the* **CHORUS**.)

TEIRESIAS. *(Laughing loudly.)* Foolish girl!

> *(Silence.* **CREON** *steps out of the* **CHORUS**, *followed by* **HAEMON** *and* **EURYDICE**.)

ISMENE. You killed her.

CREON. I didn't touch her.

ISMENE. Doesn't matter. She's dead, and it's your fault.

CREON. They're dead, too.

ISMENE. It's all your fault. Dead and gone.

CREON. You're not alone here. You think I wanted this to happen? Lose all the family I had?

ISMENE. I'm still here.

CREON. The gods have abandoned us now.

ISMENE. My sister is dead. My brothers are dead. My mother is dead. My father is dead. What good are gods if they cannot save my family?

CREON. They are not infallible.

ISMENE. So Haemon and Eurydice's deaths were simply a divine mistake?

CREON. I am not above the law. There was no choice to Antigone's death beyond how it happened.

ISMENE. So you chose the law over your own kin.

CREON. I have to keep order somehow. When Eteocles and Polynices died, they left this kingdom in turmoil.

ISMENE. That doesn't change the fact that you sacrificed your wife and son and niece in the process.

CREON. I am bound to this throne, whether I like it or not. I can't throw away precedent for the sake of my own wants.

ISMENE. Precedent doesn't matter when there are lives at stake.

CREON. This is my kingdom now.

HAEMON. You will pay for what you have done.

ANTIGONE. It was not so hard to leave me behind before, sister.

EURYDICE. Do not let your past consume you, husband. It will only serve to harm you.

HAEMON. He took everything from me. Father doesn't deserve to live peacefully.

EURYDICE. You can't change anything now.

HAEMON. He should wallow and wither and waste away.

EURYDICE. His life should not revolve around our deaths.

ANTIGONE. They should be working. They've forgotten us before.

EURYDICE. We are lost to them. Permanently. It's different.

ANTIGONE. Creon gave us up for his beloved law. Is he not satisfied?

(**TEIRESIAS** *occasionally giggles to himself.*)

ISMENE. They're really gone.

ANTIGONE. I'm still here.

CREON. They're still here.

ISMENE. It's not the same.

HAEMON. I'm still here.
CREON. They're still here.
ISMENE. It's not the same.
EURYDICE. I'm still here.
CREON. They're still here.

(Silence.)

Do they leave us?
ISMENE. I don't know.
CREON. They came back. They have to leave somehow.
ISMENE. I don't know.
CREON. They can't stay here forever.
ISMENE. I don't know.

*(Silence. **TEIRESIAS** occasionally giggles.)*

We thought we could rule the world. She wanted to be king. I'd be her co-ruler, her sister king. She knew Eteocles and Polynices were too warrior-like to rule. They would be our generals. We four, a happy family atop a happy Thebes.

(Beat.)

Obviously, that didn't work out the way she planned.
ANTIGONE. You never had the strength to be king, Ismene. You'd be useless to me. And I you.
EURYDICE. Calm, child. She cannot hear you.
CREON. I... I'm sorry.
ISMENE & ANTIGONE. What for?
CREON. I'm sorry.
ISMENE, ANTIGONE & HAEMON. What for?
CREON. I'm sorry.
ISMENE. What for?

(Silence.)

CREON. Why did she...hang herself?
ISMENE. You know.
CREON. I know?

ISMENE. I know.
CREON. You know?
ISMENE. You know.
CREON. We're not all righteous like she is.
ISMENE. Was. She's a thing of the past now.
ANTIGONE. Is that all I ever was to you? A thing?
ISMENE. I – you – we need to move on.
CREON. On? Where?
ISMENE. It's –

(Beat.)

She's not the only one here.
CREON. Here. Yes.

(Beat.)

They're here, too.
TEIRESIAS. Fate-bound. Trapped echoes.
ISMENE. Can they be freed?
CREON. Freed. How?
EURYDICE. We are not what / we were.
HAEMON. You will join me / in this hell.
ANTIGONE. Leave us in the past. Move on.
TEIRESIAS. *(Laughing maniacally.)* Fools!
ISMENE. Shut up!
EURYDICE. Listen, girl. We are here to help you.
ANTIGONE. *(Darkly.)* So you found your backbone.
EURYDICE. She must learn to move on.
ANTIGONE. I thought she already had forgotten me. She betrayed Polynices. Why should she care about me?
EURYDICE. Antigone –
HAEMON. And what of Father? Should he be allowed to forget his mistakes?
EURYDICE. He should learn.
HAEMON. From who? Death is a poor teacher.
EURYDICE. His pain will bring him strength.

HAEMON. I don't want him to be stronger! I want him to suffer!

EURYDICE. He is in agony! He will die of it if we are not careful.

HAEMON. Let him die!

TEIRESIAS. Children!

ISMENE. *(Confused.)* What?

TEIRESIAS. Shadows' echoes.

CREON. What?

EURYDICE. You're torturing the poor man!

HAEMON. What do I care?

ANTIGONE. Can we speak to them?

EURYDICE. Teiresias is our only bridge to the living.

HAEMON. Father never cared for our thoughts. Why should we try to reach him now?

EURYDICE. We need to warn them. Force them to keep going.

TEIRESIAS. *(Laughing.)* Lost shadows. Children!

ISMENE. *(Confused).* What?

(Beat.)

CREON. Your father – brothers – they left me nothing. A shaky foundation for my rule. I didn't want any of this. They weren't supposed to die and leave me here. Alone. With them. But without anyone. I cobbled together a law full of holes and fallacies and half-baked truths. It may not have been just, but it defined right and wrong.

(Beat.)

At least, I thought it did.

ISMENE. We are beyond the law. It doesn't matter. They still haunt us.

ANTIGONE. It's too late, sister.

ISMENE. Why aren't they leaving?

TEIRESIAS. Fool! They will never be free!

ISMENE. Why not? They don't belong here!

TEIRESIAS. They will never be free.

ISMENE. I have to let her go! I have to!
TEIRESIAS. She will never be free.
ANTIGONE. / You need to move on.
ISMENE. I need to move on!
CREON & EURYDICE. You can't.
ISMENE. You too, uncle? After all this?
CREON. You can't.
ISMENE. I need to.
HAEMON. / You can't.
CREON. You can't. Trust me.
ISMENE. I can't. You killed her.
TEIRESIAS & HAEMON. You will never be free.
ISMENE. What?
TEIRESIAS. You will never be free.
EURYDICE. Haemon! What are you doing?
HAEMON. Father must pay for what he has done to me.
ANTIGONE. What about Ismene?

> *(Beat.* **HAEMON** *and* **EURYDICE** *return to the* **CHORUS.***)*

ISMENE. Why?
CREON. It's not that easy.
ISMENE. It should be.
CREON. Look, kid. They're gone.
ISMENE. They're right here.
CREON. They're – I had to follow the law. You know that. But I gave her a way out. She –
TEIRESIAS. Fool!
CREON. I know. I am. She chose her path. Now she's paying the price. And you are too. I am. *(Indicating* **HAEMON.***)* He is. *(Indicating* **EURYDICE.***)* She is. We all are. Love does funny things to a person. Compromises his position. Makes him self-destruct. I bent over backwards for your sister, but she wouldn't take anything I gave. She had to be a martyr. She killed Haemon and Eurydice. I didn't. This is all her fault.

ISMENE. Liar!

> (**TEIRESIAS** *laughs.*)

CREON. It's her fault. Hers.

ISMENE. You killed her.

CREON. I didn't touch her. She killed them.

ISMENE. She didn't do anything!

CREON. Liar!

ISMENE. You killed her!

CREON. You killed her!

TEIRESIAS. *(Laughing.)* Fools!

CREON. You didn't help her. She was alone. What could she do?

ISMENE. I was there. She refused me. And I – But I refused her first.

> *(Beat.)*

You pushed them away. All they had was her. And you killed her.

CREON. I followed the law. She had to face the consequences. And so do I.

> *(He leaves the stage.* **TEIRESIAS** *observes him. A drum rings out.)*

TEIRESIAS. One more dead.

> (**CREON** *and* **TEIRESIAS** *return to the* **CHORUS.***)*

ISMENE. Antigone?

ANTIGONE. I'm here.

ISMENE. You're stuck here. How did you get here? Why are you here?

> *(Beat.)*

I did this to you. This is my fault. You should be free. I need to set you free. I need to let you go. You said you could face the punishment without me. You wouldn't let me help you. What happened? I promised you that I'd be there for you, and I broke that promise. It's my fault. My fault. My fault. How can I free you? I… Remember when we were children? When we were kings? We don't have our kingdom anymore. But I remember. We ruled this little world. Our brothers humored us as generals. Why can't we go back? I want to go back. We were happy then. This nursery was all the world we needed. It's too small for us now. You deserve that great big world outside. Go. Take it. It's yours. All yours. I won't stand in your way anymore.

ANTIGONE. This is your kingdom now. Your responsibility. I cannot be your compass. You must navigate this future alone. And you alone can change it for the better. Draw your own map. From there you can create the world you dream of.

> *(She falls back into the* **CHORUS.** *The* **CHORUS** *approaches and absorbs* **ISMENE.***)*

CHORUS. *(Chanting or singing.)* Ismene waited.
ISMENE. Creon was too late.
CREON. Hesitation has forced their hands.
TEIRESIAS. The walls echo again
HAEMON, EURYDICE & TEIRESIAS. and again
ISMENE, CREON & ANTIGONE. and again.
TEIRESIAS. Nothing / *(Beat.)* will change.
ISMENE & ANTIGONE. *(Whispering.)* Nothing...
TEIRESIAS. The players stay the same.
ANTIGONE. Antigone will die fighting.
HAEMON. Haemon will die for her.
EURYDICE. Eurydice will die for him.
TEIRESIAS. Teiresias will see all.
CREON. Creon will be too late.
CHORUS (EXCEPT ISMENE). And Ismene?
ISMENE. Will wait.

> *(Fade to black.)*

End of Play

MEMORIES OF VICHY

Samuel Kaplan

MEMORIES OF VICHY by Samuel Kaplan of Troupe 5869 at Denver (Colorado) School of the Arts was presented in a staged reading as part of the Thespian Playworks program, sponsored by Concord Theatricals, at the 2019 International Thespian Festival on June 29, 2019. The production was directed by Stewart Hawk, with dramaturgy by Judy GeBauer. The stage manager was Nadia Fryer. The cast was as follows:

AMELIE	Maddy Considine
ADULT AMELIE / MAMA	Chloe Maharg
ELOUISE	Annie Clepper
CECILE	Paige Kauffman
ANTOINE	Robert Cameron Smith
NAZI 1	DJ Tomalin
NAZI 2	Kyle Reese
MR. MOULIN	Owen Myers
ESTHER	Elizabeth Vasquez
ESTHER'S MOTHER	Zoe Necowitz

CHARACTERS

- **AMELIE** – Young, naive girl who has grown up in a small town in France. She is curious, passionate, and unafraid to speak her mind.
- **ADULT AMELIE** – Narrator. She is middle-aged and helps connect the story to present day. Also plays:
- **MAMA** – Amelie's mother. She is strict but kindhearted. She always puts family first, no matter the consequences.
- **ELOUISE** – Mature, intelligent twenty-year-old woman. She likes following the rules but still gets along with her sister, Cecile, who doesn't.
- **CECILE** – Fun-loving, expressive eighteen-year-old sister of Elouise. She always means well, but she has a short temper.
- **ANTOINE** – Amelie's brother. He is ambitious, opinionated, and not afraid to speak his mind.
- **NAZIS 1 & 2** – Soldiers that bring Amelie, Cecile, and Elouise into custody. They are drunk with power and immature.
- **MR. MOULIN** – Schoolteacher who agrees with ideologies of the Nazi Party. He becomes the town judge when the government falls.
- **ESTHER** – Classmate of Cecile. She is Jewish but has been passing as a Christian for five years.
- **ESTHER'S MOTHER** – Like Esther, she is Jewish but passing as a Christian for five years.

AUTHOR'S NOTES

Memories of Vichy is based on a story my grandmother told me about Nazis invading her small hometown of Clermont-Ferrand in France. The character Amelie is based on her. This play, written in 2019, is intended to highlight the ideological similarities between anti-Semitism in the 1940s and xenophobia, particularly toward Mexican immigrants, in 21st-century America.

Scene One

(The play is set in a small city called Montferrand, a short while after Germany invaded and occupied France. Although the play is written in English, the characters are French. **AMELIE** *is eight, wearing a long, white, floral dress.* **CECILE** *is an eighteen-year-old woman.* **CECILE***'s sister,* **ELOUISE***, is twenty years old. Both are wearing blood-red nail polish, expertly-applied makeup, and are very fashionably dressed, fitting the mold that French women were expected to fit. They live in what was once a large middle-class house that has since been turned into apartments.* **AMELIE** *lives with her family in the apartment below the sisters.)*

(Lights up. Stage right, there is a small apartment living room. Upstage facing the audience is a casement window. Upstage is a couch, and stage right is a small table with chairs and some flowers in a vase. **ELOUISE** *stands at the open window.* **AMELIE** *is seated on the couch with* **CECILE**. **ADULT AMELIE** *stands center stage.)*

ADULT AMELIE. I was eight when I first saw what the Nazis were capable of. It was summertime. Just a few weeks after France had fallen to the German army and soldiers had occupied the northern part of France. Due to a treaty, the French government kept control over the southern parts of France under German supervision. This was called Vichy France. I lived in a small city in this part of France with my family. We shared a cramped apartment. Above us, there were two older sisters who lived with their mother and father. Cecile was eighteen years old, and Elouise was twenty. These women were beautiful, stylish, fun, and I adored them so much. I followed them everywhere, but they never seemed to mind.

ELOUISE. Hey, Amelie?

AMELIE. Yes?

> *(She looks to* **ELOUISE***, while* **ADULT AMELIE** *exits.)*

ELOUISE. Come here and look at the sunset with me; it's beautiful.

> *(***AMELIE** *gets up from the couch and runs to the window.)*

AMELIE. You're right, it is.

> *(She smiles, looking out the window, admiring the sky.* **CECILE** *looks down and notices someone walking by.)*

CECILE. Oh, look, it's Mr. Moulin from the Lycee! Hello, Mr. Moulin! Say hello, Amelie.

AMELIE. Hello!

> *(She waves wildly and then turns away from the window to ask:)*

Why is he wearing that funny beret? He looks silly. It's two times the size of his head.

CECILE. It's part of the uniform for the new police force.

AMELIE. What new police force?

CECILE. The Germans have started their own police force called the Milice, and their officers are wearing those uniforms. They aren't the same as the Gendarmes. They are supposed to enforce the new laws.

ELOUISE. Yeah, Mr. Moulin from the Lycee. The history teacher. I remember him. He loved talking about the French aristocracy and the old France. The "real France" he called it.

*(**CECILE** approaches the window to join them.)*

Cecile, you don't think he is actual–

> *(**CECILE** gives **ELOUISE** a look, and she stops talking.)*

AMELIE. *(Noticing **CECILE**'s red nail polish.)* I wish I could wear red nail polish like you, but Mama says I'm not old enough.

CECILE. Well – your mother doesn't have to know.

> *(**AMELIE** makes a worried face, but one can tell she wants to say yes.)*

ELOUISE. Cecile, her mother will clearly see the bright-red poli–

> *(**CECILE** interrupts her.)*

CECILE. Elouise, it's fine, how about…we just paint her toes.

> *(She and **AMELIE** share a smile, and they move to the couch. **CECILE** begins to paint **AMELIE**'s toes. The lights dim, but one can still see the actors onstage. **ADULT AMELIE** returns.)*

ADULT AMELIE. It was small gestures like these that meant the world to me. We spent many summer afternoons in their apartment. They would talk about clothes and makeup and boys. When we were bored, we would look out the window at the people passing by. Sometimes we would play a game and make up stories about someone. Each of us would take turns adding to the story. It helped pass the long, hot summer days. I wasn't very good at it, but they still encouraged me to play along. Maybe it was because I was young and I distracted them from the war. In a way, I think I provided them hope for the future.

> *(The lights brighten, and **ADULT AMELIE** puts on an apron, now portraying **MAMA**. She moves to the doorway of the apartment, knocks, and enters. **CECILE** jumps in front of the girls so **ELOUISE** can put **AMELIE**'s shoes back on.)*

MAMA. Hello, girls, how are you?

> *(***AMELIE** *has one shoe on, and she is trying to hide her exposed foot.)*

CECILE. Hello, madame! We are well, thank you. And you?

MAMA. Amelie, what are you doing?

AMELIE. Oh, hello, Mama! I was uh… I was uh…

ELOUISE. Sorry, ma'am. We wanted to paint her toes. Amelie said no, but we told her she would look pretty.

> *(She turns and winks at* **AMELIE.** **MAMA** *gets a frustrated look on her face, but sighs because she, too, is fond of the girls.)*

MAMA. All right. We'll just have to wash it off after dinner. Amelie, go downstairs and help your brother.

AMELIE. OK, Mama.

> *(She trudges downstairs.)*

MAMA. Which reminds me, would you girls like to join us? Antoine has prepared a large cassoulet.

ELOUISE. That would be lovely, ma'am. Thank you. Our parents won't be home until dark, I'm afraid. They are staying late at the bakery again. The Nazis have been taking our flour, so they have to do what they can to serve everyone.

MAMA. That's unfortunate. If you ever need anything, we are always just down the stairs.

CECILE. Thank you, ma'am. We appreciate your generosity.

> *(They all head out the door, and the lights dim.)*

Scene Two

(When the lights come up, the couch and the table have changed places. **ANTOINE** *is seated at the table, looking down. The flowers are gone from the table and in their place is a large bowl.)*

AMELIE. Is Papa at work?

ANTOINE. Unfortunately.

(He doesn't look up from his food.)

AMELIE. I don't understand why he works so late all of a sudden. What is he –

*(**MAMA** *enters with the girls.)*

MAMA. Enough, Amelie, not now. Make some space at the table for the girls.

ANTOINE. No, you still haven't told us what Father is up to. Why has he started wo–

MAMA. *(Wincing.)* Why don't you greet Cecile and Elouise? Where are your manners?!

ANTOINE. *(Stands up.)* Sorry, Mama. Hello, Cecile, Elouise.

*(**AMELIE** *giggles. They all sit down to eat.* **MAMA** *serves everyone.)*

So, Amelie, I noticed your toes are painted.

(He smirks at **CECILE.***)*

Did Mother approve?

MAMA. I didn't, as a matter of fact. But that's all right. We will just have to take it off tonight.

AMELIE. But Mama, come on, please! Can't I just keep it for one day?

MAMA. No, Amelie. I'm sorry, but you're much too young to be wearing that sort of thing. End of discussion.

ELOUISE. So sorry again, ma'am.

(She glares at **CECILE,** *who just smiles in return.)*

MAMA. Don't worry about it, girls, you meant well. I'm so glad Amelie has friends like you. You're the older sisters she never had, and I can't thank you enough for that.

CECILE. We love spending time with Amelie. There's no need to thank us.

(She winks at **AMELIE.** **AMELIE** *giggles.)*

MAMA. So, girls, besides your flour shortage, how are your parents? How's the bakery?

CECILE. They are well, just tired. Times are just getting a little tough, but our parents will manage...

(Beat.)

...They always do.

AMELIE. Could we go there tomorrow morning? I really want a croissant or a new baguette; everything we have is stale.

*(***MAMA**, **CECILE**, *and* **ELOUISE** *wince.)*

CECILE. I'm afraid there isn't much. Most of the nice things are taken by the German soldiers.

ELOUISE. That's why business is so bad. They just need to make more for the Germans and with all these restrictions...

*(***ANTOINE** *clears his throat and side-eyes* **AMELIE**, *hinting to* **MAMA** *she probably shouldn't be here for the conversation to follow.)*

MAMA. Amelie, why don't you go get ready for bed.

AMELIE. Mama, please!

MAMA. You can come back when you're finished, but it's getting late.

*(***AMELIE** *leaves the room and closes the door, but then crouches to listen through the crack on the ground.)*

ELOUISE. You know...

(She laughs.)

Once in a blue moon we do get leftovers from the bakery when the Nazis get bored of baguettes and pastries. It's funny, I told my parents that *this* would happen, but no one wanted to listen to me.

(**ANTOINE** *looks up and frowns.*)

CECILE. We just never thought it would be this bad.

ELOUISE. No, *you* didn't think. I told Mother and Father that we should leave before they arrived. Look where we are now.

ANTOINE. And, where are you now? Your parents are collaborators!

MAMA. Antoine!

ELOUISE. *(Sadly, looking down.)* No, it's OK. He is right.

ANTOINE. How can they make bread and croissants for the Nazis!

CECILE. The Germans are forcing us to! Do you want them to refuse? Then what?

ANTOINE. Listen, I get that you didn't realize the severity of the situation, but people are dying, and you are aiding these…these murderers. Refusing is always an option.

CECILE. I don't see you refusing! What are you doing to stop the Germans?

ANTOINE. I'm – *(Sighs.)*

Have you heard the news? The radio was busy today.

(**AMELIE** *starts picking off her nail polish.*)

MAMA. Antoine, I told you to bury that damn thing. We can't let the Nazis find out we have it, let alone the fact that you listen to the English news.

ANTOINE. I will, I will, but apparently the Germans have been sending the Jews in Germany and in Eastern Europe away to "labor camps."

ELOUISE. It's not just Jews. Some of my friends heard that, in Germany, they have been sending away just about anyone that breathes wrong to labor camps. People often never come back.

CECILE. At least we're not there.

(They sit in silence, contemplating.)

ANTOINE. Not yet. But how long until it comes here? It's just a matter of time.

MAMA. Hush, Antoine. The Germans won't treat the French like that. We're Europeans!

ANTOINE. It doesn't matter that we are French. What matters is what we do.

(He pulls a flyer out of his pocket.)

I was given this today. I'm thinking of joining.

MAMA. *(Snatches it out of his hand and looks alarmed at the paper.)* Antoine, no –

*(**AMELIE** stops picking at her nail polish and leans closer.)*

ANTOINE. Just hear me out, OK? There are people dying, going hungry, being *imprisoned*. The Germans are taking our food, and it is only a matter of time before they start taking people away here as well. Look at Cecile and Elouise. Their parents are being forced to cook for the Germans.

*(**CECILE** and **ELOUISE** look at each other.)*

MAMA. You cannot join the Resistance! It's too dangerous!

ANTOINE. Too dangerous? Look around! Living here is dangerous. We have this…regime, marching around town. Elouise, you said they are taking away just about anyone in Germany, right…right?

ELOUISE. …Yeah.

ANTOINE. *(To* **MAMA**.*)* How long do we have until it's like that here? We have to act now, before it's too late.

MAMA. Antoine, I understand that it's upsetting what's happening to the Jews but… We're not Jewish, we have nothing to worry about.

ANTOINE. Nothing to worry about? People, Mother, *people* are dying every day. Sure, maybe it's not you, or me, or hell, even Amelie. But what if it was?

MAMA. But it's not.

CECILE. I think what Antoine is trying to say is that what if it was, and people you knew did nothing but stand by and watch.

MAMA. Cecile, I'm sorry, but this really doesn't concern you.

ANTOINE. There's a meeting tonight.

MAMA. Absolutely not.

ANTOINE. I was on the fence on whether I should go or not.

(He gets up and grabs his coat.)

You've convinced me.

MAMA. Antoine, don't you dare walk out that door.

ANTOINE. I'm going.

MAMA. Please...

(ANTOINE slams the front door. AMELIE gasps, and MAMA and the girls look at the door AMELIE is hiding behind.)

Amelie...is that you?

(AMELIE jumps up, scared.)

AMELIE. No...

(She runs away to her room. The adults at the table hear her.)

MAMA. *(Quietly.)* Girls, I think it's best if you go home. I'm so sorry for tonight.

ELOUISE. It's all right, ma'am. Thank you so much for dinner. Goodnight.

CECILE. Goodnight. Say goodnight to Amelie for us.

MAMA. Of course.

(The girls exit, leaving MAMA alone at the table. She slumps, looking at the front door. After she realizes ANTOINE is not returning, she begins to clean up the table. Lights fade. MAMA exits.)

Scene Three

(When the lights come up, we are now in the sisters' apartment. **ELOUISE** *enters in a new dress to find* **CECILE** *and* **AMELIE** *in new clothing, sitting by the window.* **ELOUISE** *starts tidying up around the room.)*

CECILE. OK, Amelie, it's too hot to do anything. Do you see that woman there, sitting on the bench?

AMELIE. Yes.

CECILE. What's her story? What is she doing?

MAMA. *(Calling up.)* Amelie! I'm off to the store! Do you want anything?

AMELIE. No, thank you, Mama.

MAMA. OK, be safe today!

ELOUISE. We will!

CECILE. OK, Amelie, what's her story?

AMELIE. Uh, well, she was grocery shopping, and she has bad, naughty children, and she is very angry at them, so she bought bad food like lentils, cellar vegetables, and soup and pieces of meat with large bits of fat on them. Now she is waiting for the bus so she can go home to yell at them.

(She looks embarrassed, but **CECILE** *smiles.)*

ELOUISE. *(Heads over to the window.)* Good job. OK, see him?

(She points to a man in the audience.)

AMELIE. Yes...

ELOUISE. He's a spy from England! But his wife is angry he has been gone so long, and she is starting to think he's having an affair because she doesn't know he is a secret agent.

(She points to a woman in the audience.)

See her? She is his wife spying on him! She just learned that he is a spy, and now she is mad because he lied to her!

AMELIE. Oh! Good job! But I have a twist for your story!

CECILE. *(Walks over to the window.)* Do tell.

AMELIE. She is a spy too! She is trying to find traitors, but she fell in love with him not knowing he is a spy, and now she is trying to live a double life of spy and wife!

CECILE. That was on the beam! You're getting better at this.

> (**AMELIE** *giggles and looks back out the window, where she spots two Nazi soldiers patrolling the streets.*)

AMELIE. Who are those men in the gray coats, and why are they wearing black helmets? Are those guns?

ELOUISE. It's nothing. They are just the police officers we mentioned, remember? Don't worry.

AMELIE. Are they the Nazis you were talking about yesterday, the men taking people to...

> *(Trying to remember the name.)*

Labor camps?

> (**CECILE** *winces.*)

ELOUISE. Amelie! You weren't supposed to be listening. You are too young to be worrying about this.

AMELIE. I'm old enough! I'm over a meter tall now.

ELOUISE. *(Trying to change the subject.)* Already? You are growing up so fast! Still, you shouldn't be worrying about it.

AMELIE. *(Unaware of* **ELOUISE**'*s attempt.)* It looks like they have eggs on their heads.

> (**CECILE** *starts laughing, and* **AMELIE** *starts giggling while* **ELOUISE** *gasps.*)

Broken, black rotten eggs!

ELOUISE. Where did you learn that from?

AMELIE. Antoi–

> *(From offstage, the* **NAZIS** *yell at the girls:)*

NAZI 1. *(Offstage.)* Leise sein!

(**AMELIE** *sticks out her tongue at them. The girls lean out the window, looking down.*)

CECILE. They're coming toward the house!

(*There is a loud knocking and then the sound of a door crashing open.*)

ELOUISE. Amelie, why did you do that!

AMELIE. I thought they wouldn't hea–

CECILE. Never mind that now!

(*The* **NAZIS** *arrive at the door of the apartment, and they pound on it. After a long pause,* **CECILE** *moves to the door. She takes a breath and opens the door. The* **NAZIS** *storm in.*)

NAZI 2. (*With a thick German accent.*) You think it is funny to laugh at us and mock us?

(*They smile and leer at the girls and look them up and down. The girls look down.*)

NAZI 1. (*Also with an accent.*) Well! Say something! It's not funny now, is it?

ELOUISE. No, monsieur, we weren't laughing at y–

NAZI 1. (*Interrupting her.*) Don't talk back to us. Show your superiors respect!

CECILE. (*Scoffs, steps up.*) Our superiors? I –

ELOUISE. Cecile, please we are already in a l–

NAZI 1. I have heard enough of this! Put them in the truck.

AMELIE. No please, I'm sorry, I'll...

(*The lights dim as* **NAZI 1** *picks up* **AMELIE** *and* **NAZI 2** *escorts the sisters, threatening them with his gun.* **ADULT AMELIE** *comes back onstage.*)

Scene Four

ADULT AMELIE. They loaded us into a van, and they took us with numerous other people to the Hotel de Ville. That was where the city government was and where the Germans were headquartered. We were led into a large room with many benches and a large, tall desk, similar to a judge's podium. When we walked in, we found a girl, Esther, who Cecile knew from school and who had shared several classes with her. Esther was with her mother.

> *(While* **ADULT AMELIE** *is speaking, the actors come onstage and set up the scene. There are two* **NAZIS** *in the back of the room. The girls,* **ESTHER,** *and her* **MOTHER** *are seated in the front row of benches in front of the large desk.* **ADULT AMELIE** *exits.)*

CECILE. Esther, what are you doing here?

> **(ESTHER** *is crying and looks up and shrugs.)*

(Whispers.) Do you know what they are going to do to us?

(Beat.)

Esther, say something!

ESTHER. My mother and I were just going to the market when people began pointing at us and the Germans stopped us and threw us into a van; we didn't even do anything wrong. I think my mother is hurt.

> **(ESTHER'S MOTHER** *is holding her arm and looks to be in great pain.)*

MR. MOULIN. *(Entering, looking around.)* Well, what have we here today?

NAZI 1. We picked up these girls earlier today. They were mocking our soldiers.

> *(Pointing at* **ESTHER** *and her* **MOTHER.***)*

NAZI 1. These two are Jews. Their neighbors pointed them out to us. They have no papers.

MR. MOULIN. All right, well let's deal with the easy case. Bring the mother up first.

> (**ESTHER'S MOTHER** *is roughly grabbed and carried to the desk. She cries out in pain when she is grabbed.* **NAZI 1** *then gives* **MR. MOULIN** *paperwork.* **MR. MOULIN** *reviews the paper quietly. He looks up.*)

You and your daughter are accused of being Jews. You were reported by your neighbors and taken into custody this afternoon, correct?

ESTHER'S MOTHER. No, please monsieur. We are Catholic. This is some sort of mistake.

MR. MOULIN. We don't make mistakes.

ESTHER. *(Interrupting him.)* Monsieur Moulin, please, you know us. I attended the Lycee. You know it was run by nuns. You taught me history. You've… You've known my family for a long time. We've been going to mass with you for many years now.

MR. MOULIN. Quiet! When I want to hear you speak, I will ask you to speak. Send the mother to Drancy. I've had enough of this.

> (**NAZI 1** *grabs* **ESTHER'S MOTHER** *to escort her away.*)

ESTHER'S MOTHER. No! Please! You can't do this! She's my daughter! I want to be with my daughter!

> (**ESTHER** *tries running after her but is stopped by* **NAZI 2.**)

ESTHER. Mother, no! Let go of me! You can't do this! Monsieur Moulin, please just hear me out.

(She is crying.)

I promise we aren't Jewish.

MR. MOULIN. *(Sternly, getting frustrated.)* Bring her up.

> (**ESTHER** *is escorted up.*)

Your family only started going to mass five years ago, Esther. Why is that? You and your family must have "converted" then. But the whole town knows you're Jewish. We've always said so, and it is obvious by your nose, the color of your skin, and your hair that you are Jewish.

ESTHER. But Monsieur Moulin, I swear! We are Catholic!

MR. MOULIN. No one in this town knows your grandparents! Why is that? You are not from here. Your last name isn't even French. Rosenthal? It's German!

ESTHER. We're from Alsace.

MR. MOULIN. Why, there isn't even a crucifix in your living room. I know. I was there, remember? We cannot have you and your...your family ruining the purity of France. You can't simply wash the Jew away.

(He scoffs.)

You cannot hide bad blood. It finds a way out. Send her to Rivesaltes. I think she will be more useful there.

ESTHER. No! No! Please, Monsieur Moulin! Please! I took your history class at the Lycee!

*(Calling to **CECILE**.)* Cecile! Help us. Tell him! I was in class with you. Please. Help us! Help us! I don't want...

*(She gets carried offstage by **NAZI 2**. The girls look on helplessly. **AMELIE** starts crying.)*

NAZI 1. Up, now.

*(**MR. MOULIN** nonchalantly gestures for the girls. **NAZI 2** returns, and he and **NAZI 1** approach the girls. They grab the older girls and escort them up to the desk. **AMELIE** follows, crying. **CECILE** tries to comfort **AMELIE**.)*

MR. MOULIN. Now, what do we have here? Ah yes, the two lovely Bernard girls. So nice to see you both again. I can see you are no less pretty than you were in class. And who is this lovely little girl? Why are you crying? There's nothing to be afraid of.

ELOUISE. This is Amelie, monsieur. She is the girl I was telling you about. She lives in the apartment below us. You remember her right, from the other day, when we waved at you? Amelie, say hello to Monsieur Moulin.

AMELIE. *(Looking at her feet and murmuring.)* Hello, monsieur.

>*(A **NAZI SOLDIER** brings **MR. MOULIN** a stack of papers. **MR. MOULIN** reads them quickly. He looks up.)*

MR. MOULIN. Hello, Amelie, it is nice to officially meet you. It seems there must be some mistake here. You are all accused of mocking German soldiers. I know you girls from class. You would never do such a thing. Am I correct?

ELOUISE. The Germans accused us of laughing at them, but we weren't, we swear! We were only la–

NAZI 1. No, they w–

MR. MOULIN. Enough, my dear friend, there is nothing to argue about. I will get to the bottom of this. Amelie, please come here. Girls, you can go sit back down.

>*(**AMELIE** shuffles to the center of the desk and looks up at **MR. MOULIN** while the sisters sit back down reluctantly.)*

Amelie, can you please tell me what happened?

AMELIE. *(Points to the **NAZIS**.)* I thought their helmets looked like eggs. I told Elouise and Cecile, and they laughed at me for being silly. But not at them I swear. I –

MR. MOULIN. Oh, that is quite funny.

>*(He chuckles.)*

But I'm sure you didn't mean anything offensive by it.

AMELIE. *(Looking down.)* No, monsieur. I did not.

MR. MOULIN. See? It was all a big misunderstanding.

>*(To the **NAZIS**.)* These are fine French girls. I am sure they admire German soldiers very much. They are very beautiful, as you can see. Real French women are the

most beautiful in the world. I am sure they would want to make this up to you.

(*He winks at the* **NAZIS**, *and the* **NAZIS** *nod.*)

All right, you girls can go. Now, no more egghead jokes, little one.

(*He smiles and chuckles.*)

CECILE. But monsieur, what about Esther and her mother? You knew she was a good person. She was in your class.

MR. MOULIN. (*Waves her off.*) Don't worry about them. Esther and her family aren't the kind of people we want in France. They aren't really French. They are German refugees who have been hiding in France. You wouldn't believe how bad these people are. They are all greedy, and they only care about money. You're better off not thinking about them.

(*The girls look at each other.*)

AMELIE. I don't understand.

MR. MOULIN. Amelie, what we really care for is France and the people of France. All we want is to protect the people from foreigners like the Jews who don't share our same commitment to our country. Nobody likes to see parents and children separated and carted away like Esther's family. But they aren't really French. They weren't born here. They probably crossed our border illegally. The blame should be put squarely back on the shoulders of the people who broke the law in the first place. (*To* **CECILE** *and* **ELOUISE**.) How is your mother? I haven't been to her bakery in ages. Your family makes the best éclairs. I've been really wanting a good éclair for some time now. I must stop by to see them.

ELOUISE. If you want éclairs, you'll have to come in on Fridays. (*Bitterly.*) The Germans take our flour on all the other days.

MR. MOULIN. What a shame. I'll stop by Friday, then. Tell your mother I will be coming by. I can bring two handsome soldiers with me if you like.

(He looks at the **NAZIS** *and winks. The girls and* **NAZIS** *exit.* **MR. MOULIN** *exits in a different direction, back to his office.* **ADULT AMELIE** *enters.)*

ADULT AMELIE. I was eight years old when I witnessed the German invasion of my country. A few days later, Nazi flags were flying all over the city. It only took one year before Nazi soldiers, with the help of local police, would come with their trucks, knock on doors, and embark at nightfall with families in their entirety, young and old included, and all because they were wearing a yellow star. It was terrifying, even if you knew you were not and would not be targeted. After the war, as a teenager, I saw the shame and guilt that the adult population of my compatriots carry to this day in muffled tones and disguised reminiscences. I never thought such a thing would happen in America. But now that I am an older woman, I see images of families being arrested, put into trucks, separated by police and others at gunpoint. The fault is not with the immigrant families, but with Congress and presidents who, for decades, have postponed dealing with our immigration woes. Are we going to allow this to happen here and have people arrested for the fact that they have brown skin and are fleeing here for safety? Do we want to carry this guilt? Do we want to leave this heritage of guilt to our children and grandchildren when they read about these raids in their history books? Seventy-eight years ago, I first saw what the Nazis were capable of. Today we are seeing what America is capable of.

End of Play

SILENT NIGHT

Sarah Lina Sparks

SILENT NIGHT by Sarah Lina Sparks of Troupe 6826 at Orange County School of the Arts in Santa Ana, California was presented in a staged reading as part of the Thespian Playworks program, sponsored by Concord Theatricals, at the 2019 International Thespian Festival on June 29, 2019. The production was directed by Carolyn Greer, with dramaturgy by Stephen Gregg. The stage manager was Jack Cannon. The cast was as follows:

CHILD 1	Anaka Brown
CHILD 2	Sam Charney
CHILD 3	Aliya Levin
MR. ELEPHANT	Finn Connor
MOM	Mary Catherine Kain
DAD	Holland Rolapp
PAPA (MOMMA)	Tanya King
AUNTIE	Abigail Leach
MR. BEHORD	Ethan Mock

CHARACTERS

CHILD 1 – Always follows the instructions they are told. Receptive to authority.

CHILD 2 – Frightened by commotion. Understands more than the others.

CHILD 3 – Quick to hate when put in stressful situations.

MR. ELEPHANT – Calming figure guiding the children. His eyes are kind. He has large ears that are good for listening. He loves the children.

MOM – Confused by what is happening. She needs to take action. She can't imagine doing nothing.

DAD – Angered by what is happening. Tries to find answers in the dark times. Married to Papa.

PAPA – In a deep depression due to what is happening. Is barely holding it together. Married to Dad.

AUNTIE – Frightened over what is happening. Tries to find some positivity.

MR. BEHORD – Always seen dressed sharply. He has a hard time empathizing. He never stands with the group. He knows more about the situation than anyone else; however, he is completely clueless.

AUTHOR'S NOTE

All roles except Mom and Mr. Behord may be played by any gender; any pronouns may be changed to fit accordingly.

Scene One

(There are no set pieces. The stage is a shade of deadly black. In the blackout, **CHILDREN** *spread out onstage. They breathe before they speak.)*

CHILD 1. *(Confused.)* Hello?

CHILD 2. *(Frightened.)* Is anyone here?

CHILD 3. *(Angered.)* What's going on?

(They breathe. A small moment of silence.)

MR. ELEPHANT. Hello, children.

(Lights up. The set is black and barren. There is nothing onstage except for the **CHILDREN** *and* **MR. ELEPHANT**. **MR. ELEPHANT** *is holding three red balloons.)*

My name is Mr. Elephant. How are you today?

CHILD 3. Mr. Elephant? Who are you? What is that? Where are we?

CHILD 1. Hi, Mr. Elephant!

*(***CHILD 2*** holds on to* **CHILD 1**. **CHILD 2** *is frightened.* **MR. ELEPHANT** *sees the fear. He talks to* **CHILD 2**.*)*

MR. ELEPHANT. Are you afraid?

*(***CHILD 2*** does not respond.)*

It's OK to be afraid. Would you like this balloon?

*(***CHILD 2*** nods.)*

Here, I have one for each of you.

(He ties balloons around each **CHILD**'s *wrist.)*

MR. ELEPHANT. Be careful with these. Don't pop them, OK? We're going to play a fun game.

CHILD 3. What kind of game?

MR. ELEPHANT. Have you ever played the silent game?

CHILD 3. I'm really good at that game.

MR. ELEPHANT. Then, you should be great at this! Like the silent game, when you try to be silent for as long as possible, try to keep your balloon up as long as you can. Do not let it pop, OK?

CHILD 1. OK.

> (**CHILD 2** *nods. They all look at* **CHILD 3**.)

CHILD 3. Fine.

CHILD 1. Mr. Elephant, where are we?

MR. ELEPHANT. *(Trying to amuse the* **CHILDREN**.*)* At the corner of excitement and danger.

CHILD 2. Danger?

MR. ELEPHANT. Have no fear, my friends. I will be here the whole time.

CHILD 1. Mr. Elephant? What are we doing here? Where's Mrs. Smith?

MR. ELEPHANT. Children, do you feel that?

CHILD 3. Feel what?

MR. ELEPHANT. I think it is going to rain soon.

> *(Noises of a storm commence.)*

I knew it. Here it comes.

> *(As the* **CHILDREN** *are distracted and search for the source of the storm,* **MR. ELEPHANT** *pulls a scroll out of his pocket and throws it onstage as if it magically appeared. As soon as it hits the ground, the storm stops.)*

My, my, that was quite a big one.

> *(The* **CHILDREN** *are very baffled by* **MR. ELEPHANT**'s *entire existence, along with the "storm."* **MR. ELEPHANT** *points at the scroll.)*

Now, what is that?

CHILD 3. *(Very aggressively goes to see what it is before the other children can have the chance.)* It looks like a treasure map!

MR. ELEPHANT. A measure trap?

CHILD 1. Nooooooo, a treasure map. A real-life treasure map!

MR. ELEPHANT. A ginger snap?

CHILD 2. *(Giggling from* **MR. ELEPHANT***'s silliness.)* No, Mr. Elephant. A treasure map.

MR. ELEPHANT. *(Smiling because he has achieved his goal.)* Ooh. I see now. Well, what are you silly gooses still doing standing around? Let's go and find that treasure. Who's ready?

CHILD 2. Me.

CHILD 1. Me.

CHILD 3. Well, I'm ready-er.

MR. ELEPHANT. OK children, follow me, for now we embark on our quest. *(Assuming the role of flight attendant.)* Before we take off, everyone get in a line behind me. Make sure you place your hands on the shoulders of the person in front of you. Keep all hands, arms, and legs inside the vehicle at all times.

   (Beat.)

And remember, do not let your balloon pop at any time.

   (A moment of silence.)

Now, who's ready for our adventure?

CHILD 1. What kind of adventure?

MR. ELEPHANT. It's going to be the adventure of your life.

   (He begins to lead the **CHILDREN** *offstage. They are in a line with their hands on the shoulders of the person in front of them.)*

Scene Two

> (**MR. BEHORD** *walks downstage with three balloons. A single spotlight follows him. He examines the balloons, takes out a pen, clicks it, and pops each one. The spotlight goes out, followed by a wave of dark, eerie lighting. There is a silence followed by a rush of people. They are desperate, scared, angry, confused.*)

MOM. Can someone please explain what is happening? Please!

DAD. I heard it. Did you hear it? What did I hear?

PAPA. We need to find someone to help.

AUNTIE. Excuse me. Can anyone please tell me where I can find my...

MOM. I need to see my...

DAD. Where is my...

PAPA. We need to find our...

> (*The walking patterns stop.*)

AUNTIE. Child.

MOM. Child.

DAD. Child.

PAPA. Child.

MR. BEHORD. Please, everyone, calm down. We cannot have a knee-jerk reaction. We must stay calm.

MOM. Please! We are all scared to death. I need to see my kid. She's in there. My baby is in there. Please someone tell us what is going on!

MR. BEHORD. Ma'am, we are dealing with the situation.

MOM. What even is the situation?

PAPA. (*Gripping on to* **DAD.**) Please.

DAD. Is our son in danger? I demand you tell us what's going on! We have the right to know.

AUNTIE. What is happening?

MR. BEHORD. Here is what I can tell you.
>*(He leads them into darkness offstage.)*

Scene Three

(The stage now has warm lighting. **MR. ELEPHANT** *leads the* **CHILDREN** *onstage. They are lined up together as they were before.* **MR. ELEPHANT** *assumes the role of fantastic characters in order to keep the general splendor. Although the* **CHILDREN** *are happy to be with* **MR. ELEPHANT***, they are tired. They have been through a long journey already. A hint of sleep is lingering in their eyes like a distant thought.)*

CHILD 1. Did you hear that?

CHILD 3. I didn't hear anything.

CHILD 2. I'm scared.

CHILD 3. You're a baby.

CHILD 1. Mr. Elephant? Where are we going?

MR. ELEPHANT. We have to find a ship.

CHILD 1. Like a pirate ship?

MR. ELEPHANT. Exactly! You need a pirate ship in order to go on a treasure hunt.

CHILD 3. You can't just find a pirate ship.

MR. ELEPHANT. Good thing we're going to build our own.

CHILD 2. Mr. Elephant, I don't know how to build a pirate ship.

MR. ELEPHANT. I can teach you. First, we need our materials.

CHILD 1. What do we need?

MR. ELEPHANT. Three special items…I think they're somewhere around here.

(Looking at **CHILD 1.***)* You, I need you to find something to make our boat. Find the base. It needs to be good because we're going to need a sturdy, solid vessel. It should be somewhere over there. I will be here the whole time if you need help.

(CHILD 1 runs offstage in excitement to embark on their task. MR. ELEPHANT looks at CHILD 3.)

And you, I need you to find something to help us shape and fix our base. Something to make it function the way we want. It should be over there.

(CHILD 3 runs offstage in excitement to embark on their task. MR. ELEPHANT looks at CHILD 2.)

And for you, my friend, one of the most important tasks of all. I need you to find the magic that will make this ship work.

(CHILD 2 is excited but scared.)

CHILD 2. What if I can't find it?

MR. ELEPHANT. You will. I know you will.

(CHILD 2 thinks very hard. CHILD 2 thinks they know where it is.)

Go get it. If you need anything, I will be right here.

(He looks in the direction the CHILDREN ran off to. Something inside of him hurts. A dark pit is in his stomach. It weighs him down. MR. BEHORD enters and leans against the proscenium of the stage. MR. BEHORD and MR. ELEPHANT have an exchange. MR. BEHORD clicks his pen. CHILD 1 runs back onstage. They are holding one piece of white paper. MR. ELEPHANT and MR. BEHORD can see each other. The CHILDREN cannot see MR. BEHORD.)

CHILD 1. Look, Mr. Elephant. I found it. I found it!

CHILD 3. *(Running onstage, holding a pair of scissors.)* I got mine too!

MR. ELEPHANT. Excellent job, my friends!

CHILD 3. Can we start now?

MR. ELEPHANT. No, we must wait for all of our friends. And we are missing the most important part.

(They wait. Silence.)

CHILD 1. Should we be worried?

>*(They wait. Silence.* **CHILD 2** *runs onstage, happier than they have ever been. They are carrying a flashlight.)*

MR. ELEPHANT. I'm sure he will be here soon.

CHILD 2. Mr. Elephant, I got it! I thought I wouldn't be able to, but I did! I had to go through all this stuff, but I found it. I finally found it!

MR. ELEPHANT. I knew you could do it!

CHILD 1. Now, can we start?

MR. ELEPHANT. Of course! All right, first we need our base.

Scene Four

*(**MR. BEHORD** exits. **MR. ELEPHANT** observes the piece of paper, shows it to the **CHILDREN**, fiddles with it. As this happens, **MR. BEHORD** is seen holding his pen. He observes it. He plays with it. The **PARENTS** soon enter onstage. **MR. BEHORD** takes out a notecard to read from. **MR. BEHORD** turns so his back is facing the audience. The **PARENTS** stand in front of him to receive news that will change their world forever. The **CHILDREN** cannot hear or see the **PARENTS** and **MR. BEHORD**. The **PARENTS** cannot see or hear the **CHILDREN**; however, on the inside, they are constantly looking for them.)*

MOM. Why are we here? Where is my...

MR. ELEPHANT. Now, hand me our shaping device.

*(He observes the scissors. He opens and closes them, making sure they work. He shows them to the **CHILDREN**. A beat of silence.)*

MR. BEHORD. With a heavy heart, we regret to inform you...

MR. ELEPHANT. This will shape our base.

(He begins to slowly cut the piece of paper into a triangle the size of a small boat's sail. A beat of silence.)

MR. BEHORD. Your children...

*(All the **CHILDREN**'s balloons pop. They are frightened. They scream. **MR. ELEPHANT** feels a sadness rush over him, but tries to hide it from the **CHILDREN**. He drops the shipbuilding materials. As the balloons pop, the **PARENTS** are seen reacting to horrible news. It immediately hurts the **PARENTS** from the inside. The **PARENTS** are silent. There are no words.)*

CHILD 2. I'm sorry, Mr. Elephant, I didn't mean to!

CHILD 1. I don't know what happened. It just popped.

CHILD 3. You popped mine!

CHILD 1. No, I didn't.

CHILD 2. I'm sorry, Mr. Elephant.

CHILD 3. You popped my balloon! You ruined it.

CHILD 2. I didn't do it, I swear!

CHILD 1. Maybe you did it.

MR. ELEPHANT. Children, please…

MR. BEHORD. *(Looks at the notecard.)* Please understand that we offer our deepest condolences.

    (Silence.)

MR. ELEPHANT. This is no time to fight, my friends. Please. It's OK. It's not your fault.

MR. BEHORD. We place the blame on…

MR. ELEPHANT. None of you did anything wrong.

MR. BEHORD. This single person is the cause of this travesty.

    *(The **CHILDREN** look at the balloon.)*

MR. ELEPHANT. It's OK that it popped…you did nothing wrong…sometimes things just…happen.

CHILD 3. Wait! The competition…the silent contest…who won?

MR. ELEPHANT. *(Saddened.)* Nobody won today.

CHILD 1. Mr. Elephant, I'm confused.

MOM. I'm so confused.

CHILD 1. How did the balloons pop?

MOM. How could this have happened?

DAD. This is impossible!

    *(**PAPA** clings to **DAD**.)*

AUNTIE. They were all just children.

MOM. And now, they're…they're…

    *(Lighting suddenly goes out on the **PARENTS** and **MR. BEHORD**. They exit.)*

MR. ELEPHANT. *(Struggles to form his words.)* Before you met me, what can you remember?

CHILD 3. I'm really tired. I can't remember anything, Mr. Elephant.

CHILD 1. Neither can I.

> *(Silence.)*

CHILD 2. It was Christmastime.

MR. ELEPHANT. Go on.

CHILD 2. It was Christmastime, and we went to school. When my auntie dropped me off this morning, she said after school we were going to pick out a Christmas tree and decorate cookies.

CHILD 1. When are we going home?

MR. ELEPHANT. Children, you aren't going home. Not today.

CHILD 1. What do you mean?

CHILD 3. Mr. Elephant, I want to go home! Take me home!

CHILD 2. I'm scared.

MR. ELEPHANT. *(Doesn't know what to say.)* A lost soul walked into your school today...and sometimes, when people get so lost they can't remember what's good or what's bad...they...

CHILD 2. Pop...pop...pop.

MR. ELEPHANT. What?

CHILD 2. I remember...pop...pop...pop.

CHILD 1. *(Starting to remember.)* Like a balloon.

CHILD 3. Yeah, like a really loud balloon!

MR. ELEPHANT. A lost soul came to your school today, and they popped a lot of balloons.

> *(The **CHILDREN** begin to remember everything...all of it.)*

CHILD 3. No, no, no!

CHILD 2. I want to go home!

CHILD 3. I want my dads!

CHILD 1. Mr. Elephant? Was that real?

(The **CHILDREN** *don't know how to respond to the situation. There are no words.* **CHILD 2** *grabs the paper and scissors and finishes the triangle* **MR. ELEPHANT** *created.)*

MR. ELEPHANT. Friends, it is all over now.

CHILD 1. Where are we?

MR. ELEPHANT. You're safe now. I will keep you safe.

(Silence.)

CHILD 1. I want my mom.

CHILD 3. I miss Dad and Papa.

MR. ELEPHANT. Children, I'm so sorry. This should never have happened. I promise, nothing bad will happen from here on out. I won't let it.

CHILD 2. Mr. Elephant? Will we still have Christmas?

(Beat.)

You can't be sad during Christmastime.

CHILD 1. My mom and I always watched Christmas movies and cut snowflakes together that we hung all over my house. It was like it was snowing inside!

CHILD 3. Dad and Papa and me always make awesome Christmas cookies and decorate them however we want. Last year I ate so many I had to throw up, but I didn't tell anyone so then I could eat more cookies.

CHILD 2. Ewwwww.

CHILD 1. That's gross.

MR. ELEPHANT. Do you know my favorite part about Christmastime? The lights. It may be the coldest, darkest part of winter, but the lights always shine through. They fight the darkness, and they win. And it's beautiful.

(Beat of silence.)

I promise. We will have Christmas. It'll have all the movies, cookies, trees, and lights you could ever imagine.

CHILD 2. I finished the ship.

MR. ELEPHANT. *(Recognizing* **CHILD 2***'s efforts.)* Well that is just wonderful. But you're forgetting the most important part.

> *(As much as they can, the* **CHILDREN** *are beginning to understand. They don't have a choice.)*

You forgot the light. You see, our ship doesn't work plainly like this. You need energy. You need something to make it go. You need light.

> *(***CHILD 3** *holds the paper parallel to the wall.* **CHILD 2** *holds the flashlight in front of the triangle.)*

Now, let the light in.

> *(***CHILD 2** *turns on the flashlight. This creates the shadow of a sailboat on the back wall.)*

You lead the way.

> *(***MR. ELEPHANT** *gives* **CHILD 1** *the treasure map.* **CHILD 1** *shows the other* **CHILDREN** *which way to go. They sail. They move away from where they began, leaving their popped balloons on the floor. A clear beam of light is seen coming from stage left.)*

CHILD 1. Mr. Elephant, look, look!

CHILD 2. It's like the Christmas lights you were talking about!

CHILD 3. Can we go? Can we go?

CHILD 1. Please!

CHILD 2. Please!

CHILD 3. Please!

MR. ELEPHANT. Of course! We'll start our Christmas celebration right away!

> *(As the ship sails stage left, another shadow enters the spotlight. It is the clear shape of a Christmas tree. The boat meets the Christmas tree, and the* **CHILDREN** *are anxious to see what lies ahead of them. They run offstage, together.)*

Scene Five

*(The **PARENTS** enter. The lights are darker. All are still. They hold one candle each. **MR. BEHORD** is standing near them, but not with them. The **PARENTS** hum the tune "Silent Night" on a "hm." The only word of the song they sing is the word "silent." **MR. BEHORD** will not sing with them.)*

MOM. No.

PAPA. Excuse me?

MOM. No.

DAD. We are mourning our child, please…

MOM. I can't handle this any longer.

AUNTIE. Please, dear, calm down.

MOM. I will not! I will not calm down. At eight o'clock this morning, I sent my baby to school. At three, I was supposed to pick her up. They were supposed to come home. I don't want to be silent. I want to scream! I want to turn the world upside down. I want my daughter back.

AUNTIE. We all want that, dear.

PAPA. It's nearly Christmastime. That was my kid's favorite time of the year.

AUNTIE. *(Trying to cheer everyone up.)* Mine too. Just as I dropped them off today, they turned to me and said, "Have you mailed my letter to Santa yet? I don't know if the North Pole has fast shipping and it needs to get there in time."

MOM. I just…our children…they can't be…how…this isn't right. This can't be right.

(Beat.)

DAD. That man will pay for everything he's done! He has hurt all of us, the entire town, the entire country…

PAPA. Who would've thought it would hit us? What are the odds? You see these things happen on the news, you mourn for the children, for their families. You never would have thought in a million years it would hit our town…our children…

AUNTIE. Whenever I saw this on the TV, I couldn't help but think about the pain everyone must have gone through. I could never imagine it. Even now I still can't believe it. I… I can't believe that it's true. It mustn't be true. It just can't be.

MR. BEHORD. On behalf of everyone, I would like you to know we have heavy hearts. Our thoughts and prayers are with you. We hear you.

(Beat.)

MOM. You hear us? What do you hear? Do you hear the sound of my daughter sobbing when I had to tell her that the bottom bunk is going to be empty from now on? Did you hear the silence on the other side of the phone when no one knew what to say? Did you hear the children?

> *(**MR. BEHORD** takes out a notebook from his pocket to look in his notes for what to say. It is a long and thin notebook. If it is on the right angle, one might think it is a checkbook.)*

MR. BEHORD. You are not alone in your suffering.

(Some chaos erupts in the group.)

MOM. What?

DAD. What difference does that make? Our children are gone, and we want answers!

AUNTIE. What really happened? How did it happen? How could this happen?

MR. BEHORD. First, I think we should take a moment of silence and think about the lives we have lost.

MOM. No! No more silence! You talk as if I don't think about the "lives that were lost." Like I won't think about my own daughter every second, of every hour, of every day. I've thought. I've prayed. I've had my moments of silence. This is not the first time this sort of thing has happened, and how depressing is it that everyone knows it won't be the last? I am going to yell, and scream, and fight. We lost our children...our children! And I will be damned if another family must suffer the same pain we have and you do nothing about it. Until you understand what is at stake, I will not be silent.

MR. BEHORD. *(Annoyed.)* Ma'am, please quiet down.

DAD. *(Holding **PAPA**'s hand.)* No.

PAPA. No.

AUNTIE. No.

MR. BEHORD. *(Exasperatingly writes in notebook with the pen.)* Quiet!

> (**MOM** *goes up to* **MR. BEHORD**, *grabs the pen out of his hand, and throws it offstage.*)

MOM. We will not be silenced.

(Blackout.)

Scene Six

(MR. ELEPHANT is seen standing alone. Waiting. MR. BEHORD enters stage right. He holds a large bundle of red balloons and tries to give them to MR. ELEPHANT.)

MR. ELEPHANT. No. This is impossible. There must be some sort of mistake.

MR. BEHORD. This is no mistake.

MR. ELEPHANT. Please, no. I can't do this.

(MR. BEHORD hands MR. ELEPHANT the balloons, turns his back to him, and prepares to walk offstage.)

MR. BEHORD. Mr. Elephant, there is nothing I can do. I apologize.

MR. ELEPHANT. They're only children!

MR. BEHORD. You will take care of them now.

MR. ELEPHANT. No. Please, send them back! Do something!

(Beat.)

Mr. Behord! Please! I don't want any more balloons. People are suffering, can't you see? Open your eyes... open your mind...open your heart. Do anything!

(Beat.)

See how they weep. Feel their desperation, their pain. Listen. Listen to the silence. Can you hear it? The emptiness and vacancy.

(Beat.)

Now listen again.

(Suddenly, the hum of "Silent Night" is heard in the distance. Once again, the only word that is sung is "silent.")

Do you hear that? The noise is coming. And it'll come like a storm, Mr. Behord. A storm of biblical proportions. It is unavoidable, strong, and if you get in its way, it will be your demise. I guarantee you that.

> (**MR. BEHORD** *does not turn back. He tightens his tie and begins to walk offstage.*)

They're just kids. Help them. Why won't you help them?

> (**MR. ELEPHANT** *is left examining the balloons. His heart aches. He looks out desperately to the audience. He breathes. Blackout. A multitude of balloons pop, then, silence. The blackout lasts a minute longer than anyone thinks it should.*)

End of Play

www.ingramcontent.com/pod-product-compliance
Lightning Source LLC
Chambersburg PA
CBHW072019290426
44109CB00018B/2283